I AM

AFFIRMATIONS TO CREATE WEALTH

Bernard Smalls

Visualize-Affirm-Meditate

I AM Affirmations To Create Wealth

Printed in the United States of America

Published by O. Bernard Smalls

Genre: Success Motivation

PREFACE

Welcome to the journey of 'I AM'. My intention in writing this book is Spiritual-Pragmatism for the everyday person. Spiritual-pragmatism is a marriage between the spiritual and the practical, which results in exploits. I want to help you understand a simple, yet profound concept that will manifest in your success and financial freedom. The message in this book is simple yet very powerful! Here is the message; 'I AM' are the two most powerful words you can utter. Whenever you say 'I AM,' you activate the Law of Being, by declaring yourself 'To Be'. Whatever you say after 'I AM', you create in your life. So, when you make 'I AM' affirmations of prosperity, you actually create prosperity.

There is a scientific and psychological reason for this. Leading neurosurgeons have discovered that the speech center in the brain rules over all the nerves. Medical science has recently discovered that the speech nerve center has such power over the whole body. As such, simply "speaking" positive affirmations can give one control over his body. The purpose of this little book is to help you take control of your finances and prosper in life. My desires for you are your success and prosperity through the spoken word. I aim to make the 'I AM' insight simple and plain in the pages of this book. I encourage you to read the book for positive information and I encourage you to enjoy making the 'I AM' affirmations to create wealth!

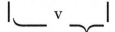

v

CONTENTS

CHAPTER 1

THE VAM CONCEPT

"I am visioning, affirming and meditating

on abundance!"

My goal in this book is to help you understand a simple, yet profound concept that will result in your financial freedom. The message is simple, yet it is very powerful! It works! 'I AM' are the two most powerful words you can speak. When you say 'I AM,' you declare yourself 'To Be'. Whatever you say after 'I AM', you create in your life. Does this include wealth? Yes! This includes wealth. That is why I entitled it 'I AM Affirmations to Create Wealth'. The power of 'I AM' is not a gimmick, but a Divine principle. This book is not about theology but practical principles that work. I am here to help you grow and prosper, not to judge your spirituality. Thus, no condemnation or judgments herein.

I want to start out on our journey by introducing to you a simple motivational process for super success. This is a principle or spiritual practice that is spiritual yet practical. I call this process VAM. VAM is a concept that emerged as an insight one day while I was making my daily affirmations. As

I was meditating, I clearly saw the word **VAM** in my inner being.

VAM

So, what is VAM? VAM is a spiritual and psychological process for producing prosperous results. I will explain this process simply and thoroughly as we move on in our journey through this book. VAM is an acronym for Visualization, Affirmation and Meditation.

My advice is that you read this book in totality because it is written purposely to create wealth in your life. Every chapter is important. I ask that you do yourself a favor and commit to finishing the journey. Commit now to finishing this book. Okay?

So, do we have a deal? Great! Let's go...

This book will expand your PROSPERITY CONSCIOUSNESS. Expanded prosperity consciousness is guaranteed to increase your personal wealth.

So your intentions are:

Developing more Right-Thinking and

Expanding your Prosperity Consciousness.

Keep these simple objectives in mind as you engage in the reading journey. *This book is going to change your life!*

THE VAM PROCESS

I have had people say; *"Bernard, affirmations just don't work! I have tried them and I am still broke!"* First of all, I fully understand where you are coming from. 'I have been there, done that and bought the tee-shirt!' There have been times that I have wondered if my affirmations were working.

In fact, that is basically why I wrote this book. I have felt the frustration of affirming with seemingly no prosperous results. That is how and why I created the VAM process. I needed answers to my dismal financial situation. I needed a workable strategy or process. Why do I call it a process? It is basically because VAM is a three-part system. Spiritual things like everything else work in the context of a process. When you understand the process and apply it, you win in life. I have personally learned that affirmations do work. But the process must be applied contextually in order to get positive results. What do I mean here? When affirmations appear to not work, it is usually a failure to apply the affirmation process in proper context. That failure to apply the principles of the process in context causes failure in life. Let me illustrate. Let's say, you are faced with a seven-step stairway to enter a hall. Implying that getting to the top takes seven steps. What if you climb four steps only? You wouldn't enter the hall. *Would you? But why?* You have not yet applied the seven-step process in context. The contextual realm of the process in my simple illustration given here is seven steps to the top, not four steps. So, if you said stairs don't work, is that really so? Process and context are important. To be totally honest with you, you will have much frustration with spirituality and life in general until you understand this. These things work by process. VAM is a simple process.

1-2-3 VAM!

You must apply the process and three steps to your thinking, and condition it into your consciousness.

Here's another thing to know. This does not happen overnight. *It is a process!* In fact, everything in life is a process. I like the word process (if you haven't noticed).

I have successfully done sales training for years. I always start out by teaching the salespeople a sales process. The ones who master and follow the process *(with some common sense)* always succeed. The ones who don't follow the process, well! They simply fail.

The same is true here. Get an understanding of the process, and you will use affirmations to create wealth. Prosperity is not luck, fate or magic, it's a process. I am here to give you tools that work, not just those that sound good! The VAM process is the pathway to wealth. VAM again is an acronym for the three-step process of Visualize, Affirm and Meditate. Memorize and release the power of VAM!

WHAT IS PROCESS?

Now, let us dig a little deeper into understanding the concept of process. Process is defined in Webster's Dictionary as a series of actions or operations conducing to an end. For example, in sales, a good sales process starts with prospecting (finding a customer) and it ends with a successful sale.

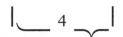

THINK!

Let's have a think-shop. I want you to get the concept of process vividly clear before we go on with this journey.

Take a moment and think of a process that you have been trained professionally, maybe at work or in college. Think!

What were the key elements of the process?

What are the main concepts?

What did you do first or last?

How many steps did the process have?

What were the steps?

What did success look like?

In everyday life, when you understand and apply the proper steps to a process, you get good results. *You make the sale.*

The same is true with spiritual practices. VAM is a process you must practice.

I have provided you with five sets of VAM affirmations for your daily workshops in the appendix section of this book. These affirmations are segmented to train and develop your right-thinking/prosperity consciousness.

APPLYING VAM! PRODUCES BAM!!

VAM is a psychological workshop for internalizing 'I AM' consciousness to create wealth.

As earlier said, VAM is an acronym for Visualize, Affirm and Meditate. The process is not difficult at all, but very powerful and effective.

THIRTY DAYS TO FINANCIAL FREEDOM

Here is how I suggest you use it. Read a chapter of this book daily over a period of thirty days. The book should become your handbook for thirty days. Simply take 10 to 15 minutes reading daily for **thirty days**, and 10 to 15 minutes going over the affirmations in the appendix. So, the workshop should take 20 to 30 minutes over thirty days. VAM affirmations applied for thirty days will cause you to experience a shift in consciousness within. Everything you get in life you get in consciousness first. The prosperity consciousness within will start to out-picture or manifest wealth in your circumstances. The key is that you engage in consistent action. You must VAM daily! You should ideally, do this first thing in the morning, while your mind is still clear. As you read each affirmation do three things:

1) **V**isualize yourself being prosperous.

2) **A**ffirm the affirmation out loud.

3) **M**editate (think) on and imagine your prosperity.

I want you to make this daily VAM practice just as much a part of your life as eating breakfast. As you do, you will be right on track in training your prosperity consciousness for manifesting success, good results, and prosperity.

VAM creates reality.

VAM creates wealth.

VAM creates BAM!!!

Now, in the next chapter let's talk about the power that shapes your life...

"Consciousness, rather than being an epiphenomenon of matter, is actually the source of matter. It differentiates into space-time, energy, information, and matter. Even though this view is an ancient view, an ancient world view, it is now finding some resonance amongst a few scientists."

--Deepak Chopra

AFFIRM:

"I AM visioning, affirming and meditating on abundance daily!"

'I AM' JOURNAL

_____

_____

_____

_____

_____

_____

_____

_____

_____

_____

_____

_____

_____

_____

_____

_____

_____

_____

CHAPTER 2
THE POWER THAT SHAPES
YOUR LIFE!

"I am open and ready to attract abundance into my life."

As we indicated in chapter one, the VAM workshops practiced daily for **thirty-days** will build in you right thinking and a prosperity consciousness. This process is no hype! No trick! No gimmick! By the way, there is no special magic in the number thirty as regarding thirty days. The thirty days is about consistency. You change your thinking (consciousness), and then your life. This right-thinking/prosperity consciousness has the power to create wealth in your life. This is because the subconscious mind is very powerful and right practices such as VAM, programs the subconscious. Everything you get in consciousness, you get in life. The VAM workshops help you develop a prosperity consciousness. Daily repetition is the key. Repeated visioning, affirming, and meditation of prosperous outcomes will eventually plant wealth into your subconscious mind like a seed sinking into the soil. When this happens, the manifestation of prosperity is the result. This is simply the law of cause and effect, or sowing and reaping.

So you ask, come on Bernard, what does cause and effect have to do with this? I am so glad you asked. To make it simple; Thinking is the cause and wealth creation is the effect. When you change your thinking, what happens?

You get it! *You change your life!* This is making sense to you now. Isn't it? VAM helps to change your thinking by sowing seeds of prosperous thinking. We will discuss this more later.

Now, let's talk about something that is so powerful and which can virtually shape your life. This concept is already working in your life, either consciously or unconsciously.

So, what is this awesome power? It's the power of 'I AM', the power of affirmation. Affirmation is the power that shapes your life. 'I AM' affirmations are already working for you because you say 'I AM' on a daily bases. That's why I say this power is already working in your life. You are already using or saying I AM! Let's simply focus your 'I AM', with regards to prosperous results. This is the power to create wealth. My message is simple; "Your words have power!" 'I AM' are two words that are filled with Infinite Power! What you say after the words 'I AM' is created in your life. 'I AM' affirmations are especially powerful because that which follows the words 'I AM' becomes your reality and is manifested in your life. So, let's activate your prosperity consciousness by making some 'I AM' affirmations:

"I am open to receiving abundance."

"I am now attracting abundance."

"I am living a life of abundance."

"I am living in the overflow."

"I am attracting money easily and effortlessly."

"I am living a life of unlimited abundance."

"I am flowing in the abundance that is all around me."

"I am affluent. I have an abundance mindset."

"I am living my life in a state of complete abundance."

"I am abundance!"

'I AM' ...

Whatever you say after 'I AM', is created in your world. I will make this statement in various ways throughout this book. The insights behind 'I AM' are profound knowledge. It is the power of 'I AM'. Let me illustrate. If you say 'I AM HAPPINESS', then life will provide you the means to have happiness. If you say 'I AM HEALTHY', the result will be health. If you say 'I AM WEALTHY', you eventually get the corresponding result of wealth.

'I AM' is not only spiritual, but it is also scientific! It is a law. This concept is based on the law of cause and effect.

CAUSE & EFFECT

This law states for every effect, there is a cause. Cause and effect is a basic law that is commonly understood.

A simple example of cause and effect is what we call the domino effect. At times, one event might trigger another event or happening, which may lead to yet another event. This is known as **the causal chain or domino effect**. When one domino falls and hits another, it knocks it into another, etc. That's cause and effect. 'I AM' is the cause, just like the first domino, while the manifestation (the falling domino) is the effect.

'I AM' is 'First Cause' and what follows is the 'effect'.

When you say 'I AM', that which follows is always shaped in your life, including prosperity. This is true because 'I AM' is your awareness of BEING, which is a creative power. You always eventually manifest that which you are aware of BEING. 'I AM' is the law of being, your awareness of being.

Once you say, I AM wealthy, you are aware of being wealthy, so you release the invisible power to create wealth. We will share more in-depth about the power of awareness later in this book. First, just realize that 'I AM' is the power to create the wealthy life you deserve, or wields the power to create wealth.

The key is to replace and disempower negative 'I WANT' and 'I NEED' affirmations with positive empowering 'I AM' affirmations. This simply takes a consistent training of the mind and the mouth. Much of this training will take place in your daily VAM workshops over the thirty days. Engage in the 30-Day trial of VAM! It will pay rich dividends!

I want to help you make the shift from negativity to 'I AM' (positivity). I want to inspire you in using the power of 'I AM' affirmations to create wealth.

FIERY DARTS -THE LAW OF OPPOSITES

Now let's talk about something that very few understand. What I am talking about is the law of opposites. The law of opposites creates a contextual field for the law of 'I AM' to operate. Let me illustrate. The moment you decide to affirm anything good or positive, everything unlike your affirmation comes into the space. This is the law of opposites, playing itself out. If you do not understand this law, you will not understand what is going on around you, and you will become very discouraged, disheartened, and disillusioned when the opposite of your affirmation appears. Scripture calls this activity the fiery darts. The shield of faith will stop them!

Only if you are clear that the world opposing you is 'I AM' agreeing with you that you can overcome these spiritual and emotional pitfalls. The law of opposites is the sure evidence that the law of 'I AM' is working. What we are saying is, after you have made positive 'I AM' affirmations, EVERYTHING unlike your desire shows up. The key is, judge not by appearances and walk by faith not by sight.

Call forth that which you want and be aware of the Law of Opposites. My advice is that; do not see the opposition as negative but as a part of the deal. An acronym for Satan I like is 'SEEING ANY THING AS NEGATIVE –S.A.T.A.N.'

The law of opposites is sure evidence that the law of 'I AM' is working. SATAN (SEEING ANY THING AS NEGATIVE) comes immediately to take out the seed of the 'I AM' that was sown. You are the sower and your 'I AM' affirmation is the seed. Just realize that everything, including the opposition to your affirmation happens for a reason. Next, we will learn about 'The Mystery of I AM'. Keep reading...

AFFIRM:

'I AM' is the power to create wealth. I AM wealthy now!

'I AM' JOURNAL

_____
_____
_____
_____
_____
_____
_____
_____
_____
_____
_____
_____
_____
_____
_____
_____
_____
_____
_____
_____
_____
_____

CHAPTER 3

THE MYSTERY OF 'I AM'

"I am attuned to the frequency of love
and abundance."

What is the mystery of 'I AM'?

I find it very interesting that the words 'I AM' are the two most powerful words in the human language. This is especially intriguing being a student of theology. I don't want to make this book deeply religious or theological, but you must understand this great mystery; God, Infinite Intelligence is 'I AM'.

You will expand your awareness of this as you continue to read this book. For now, just realize that the words 'I AM' are powerful. They are Divine.

THE MYSTERY OF 'I AM'

Now let's get some basic, practical insight into the mystery of 'I AM'. First of all, the big question to answer is why the two words 'I AM' would have so much power in our everyday lives? This mystery is what we call THE LAW OF BEING.

Here is how this law works. Saying 'I AM' makes what you are saying manifest in your life. What you are conscious of BEING will manifest in your life. It's simply The Law of BEING!

I know my teaching is a bit different from conventional tradition. I teach the psychology of the Bible. Psychology is the study of the mind. I teach right-thinking, positive thinking. That is why I call it the psychology of the Bible.

Now, I will lay a foundation for much of what we will cover later in this book. Here is a powerful thought that you must understand because it is the psychological basis of this book. First of all, whatever you say after the words 'I AM', you create or shape in your life. Whatever you say after 'I AM' also becomes your reality. The power of 'I AM' is not a religious teaching. It is rather practical psychology. It works!

There is a tremendous psychological reason for why the power of 'I AM' works. Simply said, Psychologists say that when you say the words 'I AM', you alert your subconscious mind to bring to past or manifest what you say after the words 'I AM'. If you say I AM wealthy, you will be releasing the power to create wealth. If you say I AM strong, you will be releasing the power to be strong. "Let the weak say I AM strong."

'I AM' causes you to engage in what you say afterward, even if it is the opposite of your present reality. Now think for I moment, the text did not say "let the weak say I am weak." Why? This is because, the affirmation would create weakness! **You always become your 'I AM.'** I AM is the Law of Being because when you say, 'I AM,' you are declaring yourself 'To

Be' (first person, and present tense) Now and not in the future, but Now! 'I AM' is the power of Now! In the next chapter we will learn some more about the subconscious mind. It is exciting knowledge. Keep searching...

AFFIRM:

I AM aware of BEING,
I AM!

'I AM' JOURNAL

_____

_____

_____

_____

_____

_____

_____

_____

_____

_____

_____

_____

_____

_____

_____

_____

_____

_____

_____

_____

_____

_____

CHAPTER 4

THE SUBCONSCIOUS MIND

"I am a believer in my abilities to attract financial abundance."

Discovering how to turn your thoughts into positive 'I AM' affirmations and implementing them into your daily life can take you to new heights personally, mentally and financially. The untapped power of the subconscious mind can lead you to new success in your personal and business life. In order to understand the power of your subconscious mind, you first need to understand the difference between your subconscious and your conscious mind. Jack Canfield, author of Chicken Soup for The Soul has superbly said; "To make it simple; your conscious mind is the awareness you have in the current moment. This is your awareness of your surroundings, your current thoughts and emotions, the physical sensations in your body, whether or not you're hungry, and so on. Your subconscious mind is any information that is below the threshold of your current awareness."

Mr. Canfield went on to say; "examples of your subconscious are memories, beliefs, fears, and subjective reality." Subjective simply means within.

The awesome thing with your subconscious mind is that, it is very powerful and can without your awareness, direct the course of what you do in your life. With cognizance of the power of the subconscious mind, you must learn to choose your thoughts and words effectively.

Your thoughts and words, both conscious and subconscious are creating your current experience of reality— including your level of prosperity. Well, what does 'I AM' have to do with this? I am so glad you asked...

'I AM' ACTIVATES THE SUBCONSCIOUS

The reason why this 'I AM' law works is simple, yet profound. When you say 'I AM', you alert and activate the subconscious within you. The subconscious is the spirit of man. In everyday vernacular, we call him the human spirit. This is why you can have what you say. Your words have power in them. When you say the words 'I AM', you definitely take it to another level.

You activate the human spirit when you say 'I AM'.

You actually take it to the highest or supreme levels in the invisible world. 'I AM' is positive thinking. What can be more positive than 'I AM'? Thoughts, either positive or negative are *things* of the spirit world.

Thought is a powerful part of that invisible spiritual world. Whenever you say 'I AM', you express *'thought'* that will eventually manifest in your world. Affirm now: 'I AM Prosperous'!

THOUGHTS

Thoughts are so powerful! *Think* with me for a moment.

Two of the most powerful things we can do as Homo sapiens or human beings are;

1) We can have many thoughts.

2) We can speak words.

Those may seem like normal and obvious things to do. But in the invisible world, we wield tremendous power through our thoughts and words. Here is why: **'You become what you think and talk about.'** This is spiritual law.

Did you know that thoughts are unspoken words?

Words are spoken thoughts. This is why it is important to guard your thoughts as they eventually become words. Thoughts and words are critical to your prosperity, wouldn't you agree? The key to abundant life is to have prosperous thoughts and then speak prosperous words. That is why I emphasize 'affirmation' so much. You need to continually make positive prospering 'I AM' affirmations. You can even inspire yourself and others by the practice of 'I AM' affirmations. There is prospering power in them.

I believe that the most powerful insight you will ever gain in your journey on planet earth is the Secret Power of 'I AM'. I call it *'The Secret Power'* because only a few know about it.

BEING DEBT FREE

The power of 'I AM' is the key to being debt-free. This is because it massively reprograms the subconscious mind.

If a person is in debt or people owe him money, it instills that belief of debt is in his subconscious mind. This belief must be neutralized in order to change conditions. Affirming 'I AM Debt Free' activates the subconscious to manifest debt-freedom.

To manifest debt-freedom, make this statement: "I deny debt; there is no debt in the Divine Mind. I owe no man anything but love. All my obligations have been wiped out under grace in a perfect way." Now, what is the real power to create wealth? Keep reading and you will know...

AFFIRM:

"I AM debt free! I have financial abundance."

'I AM' JOURNAL

_____

_____

_____

_____

_____

_____

_____

_____

_____

_____

_____

_____

_____

_____

_____

_____

_____

_____

_____

CHAPTER 5

THE ABILITY TO CREATE WEALTH

"I am wealthy. I attract success."

'I AM' is Creative Power!

'**I** AM' is the **Power to Create Wealth. We always need to remember that.**

Affirm: 'I AM' is the ability to create wealth.

How does 'I AM' create wealth? It is so simple yet, so profound. 'I AM' creates by the power of the spoken word.

The words 'I AM' shape your entire life. Your words frame your world. 'I AM' creates all things by saying; 'I AM THAT I AM'.

This does not make sense to the natural mind but we are dealing with a higher realm of consciousness here. We are dealing with the Law of Being. What are we talking about? The Law of BEING states; that which you conceive, believe and affirm becomes a reality in your life. When you say or affirm the words 'I AM', you release creative power. This is because when you say 'I AM' you release the power of Being. **Does this make sense?** 'I AM' is really about the power of awareness. You manifest what you are aware of being. It is critical that we understand the power of awareness and the law of being. You must be aware of being rich, then aware of being aware-of-being-rich. This is not just a play with words. It is the truth. You must be aware of being rich regardless of your present financial situation. This is the law of being.

POWER OF AWARENESS

Now let's look into the power of awareness.

Here is a simple definition of awareness; *it is the quality or state of being aware, knowledge and understanding that something is happening or exists.*

'I AM' is actually 'awareness' of being. You could not intelligently say 'I AM', if you were not aware. Is that true?

You could say 'I AM' is the power of awareness. We must understand the power of awareness and how it works. When you say 'I AM', you unleash the power of awareness. I want to say it in another way, the very words 'I AM', expresses the awareness of *'Being'*. This is also the law of deliberate creation. Some call it the law of expression. You express yourself by affirming 'I AM', don't you? So, you are now creating wealth on purpose, and with intention. If someone says; I did it intentionally, they are guilty of doing it. We must understand the power of intention. Here is a simple definition of *intention*: A determination to act in a certain way; *Resolve*, what one intends to do or bring about; the object for which a prayer, mass, or pious act is offered, a process or manner of healing, attention directed to an object of knowledge (Webster's). Intention is simply a deliberate decision. That is why we call it deliberate creation.

Let us simplify this; for example, if you say "I AM prosperous", you are saying; "I AM deliberately *being* prosperous or I AM aware of *being* prosperous. If you say "I AM healthy," You are saying; "I AM deliberately *being* healthy or I AM aware of *being* healthy. It is just that simple.

'I AM' is a deliberate choice. Bear that in mind as you read.

CREATED IN HIS IMAGE

Man was created in the Image of 'I AM'.

So you can affirm 'I AM *His* Image'. Say this out loud now; 'I AM *His* Image'. You are *His* Image. Develop your 'I AM' consciousness.

Well, what is consciousness? It is simply awareness. Remember, 'I AM' is your awareness of being. The 'I AM' consciousness means you are always aware of the power of 'I AM'. If you are conscious of something, it means you are '*Aware of being it*'. Are you not?

As we come to the end of this chapter, just remember that a person who has developed the 'I AM' consciousness understands better, and is aware of the fact that words have power and the words 'I AM' have Supreme power.

So, whatever you say after 'I AM' is shaped and created in your life. Just keep saying 'I AM'.

It will manifest in due time.

If you say 'I AM a millionaire', you are aware of being a millionaire or being rich. 'I AM' is the power of awareness. It calls things into *'Being'*. 'I AM' is and has creative power. We are created in the Image of 'I AM'.

'I AM' gives us the power and ability to create wealth.

We must understand the power of 'I AM'.

AFFIRM:

"I AM Conscious of I AM!"

'I AM' JOURNAL

CHAPTER 6
THE LAW OF BEING

"I am living my life in a state of being abundance."

N ow, let's talk about something which has a great need for insight into. That is 'The Law of Being'. 'I AM' is the power that makes all that you are aware of *being* in your life. This is the truth. No stunts or device. All that is required of you is to believe, accept and affirm *being* your desire. If you dare claim, affirm and **be** it, 'I AM' will express and manifest. This is true with all things including money, prosperity and wealth. *Do you want wealth?* You can have it. It's no big deal to 'I AM'. I AM wants you to be rich. But you must understand and accept *The Law of Being*. You must **be** rich from within first, and then you will manifest it without (on the outside). That's the message of this book! That is the Kingdom or the realm of 'I AM'. It operates from the inside out.

There has been very little understanding of the power of *being* in the life of the average individual. Schools, churches and other institutions have not majored on it yet. This is why

I'm outlining the insights on **awareness of being** in this book. So, what is the power of awareness? The power of awareness basically entails that, you are aware of *being*. Think about the word *being*. Affirm: *'I Am Aware of Being'*. First, you are aware of being, and then you are also aware of being aware. This is profound. **Your Life Is Simply An Out-Picturing of That Which You Are Aware Of Being.** Out of the abundance of the heart *(being)*, the mouth speaks. Jesus Christ taught this when *He* said; "you can have what you say if you *believe* in or with your heart".

I AM AWARE OF BEING!

Believing with the heart is equivalent to *being*. Why? You become what you believe. More so, you are what you believe with your heart or within. As being is within, so is without. Therefore, *be* it. You will effortlessly draw to yourself all that you were conscious or aware of being. Is that simple enough? You 'Be it' and then, you 'See it'. You could say 'The Me I Be Is the Me I'll see'. You **BE** it within, then you see it without. This is why reading books and listening to prosperity teaching is so important. The transformation starts from within, in consciousness.

Affirm softly: 'I AM being transformed from within!'

TRANSFORMATION WITHIN

Before you can transform your outer world, you must first renew your inner world. Here is the secret, *It Is Within!* This is called the renewing of your mind in the Bible.

To renew the mind is to train your consciousness to an awareness of the power of 'I AM' within.

Man must know 'I AM'.

You must believe in the power of 'I AM'.

BELIEVE IN 'I AM'

Unless a person discovers the power of 'I AM', which means that his consciousness is the cause of every expression of his life, he will continue seeking the cause of his confusion or problems in the sense-knowledge world of effects. He will live and wander in a mental wilderness then die in his fruitless search and not be delivered from his life's problems. The negative thinking spies who died in the wilderness typify this case in the Bible. They simply would not believe Moses! Believing in 'I AM' is the key to success in this life. Prosperity is for this life. If you don't know the power of 'I AM' now, you will live and die in poverty. It is vital that you understand and believe in the power of 'I AM'. You must believe that the power of 'I AM' is the law of being. As you do, you will enjoy prosperity and health.

Awareness of being is the first step of the journey.

Awareness is awakening.

Whatever you say after 'I AM' becomes your reality.

Awake to right living, and you will stop missing the mark of prosperity and success. Get the knowledge of 'I AM'. Get in touch with *being*... Affirm: 'I AM aware of being!'

AFFIRM:

'I AM aware of being!'

'I AM' JOURNAL

_____

_____

_____

_____

_____

_____

_____

_____

_____

_____

_____

_____

_____

_____

_____

_____

_____

_____

_____

_____

CHAPTER 7

THE DOOR OF PROSPERITY

"I am living a life of abundance."

'I AM' is the *door* of prosperity. *How could this be?* This is because whatever you say after 'I AM' is created in your life, including prosperity. 'I AM' are the words that open the door of prosperity. This is because 'I AM' is the door of prosperity!

'I AM' is the door to prosperity.

Well, what is a *door*? It is the entry way into a facility. Yet, it is also the exit. When you leave a building, you walk through the door, not through the wall. 'I AM' is the entry way into prosperity. *What am I saying here?* I am saying that when you say the words 'I AM rich', you are opening the entry or the door to a life of wealth.

THE SWINGING DOOR

Saying 'I AM poor' is *also* the exit from prosperity and the entry way into poverty and lack. This door works both ways. You can enter prosperity or exit it by the power of 'I AM'. Imagine a swinging door, like the door on the old saloon in a western.

It swings in and out. It swings in the direction of your push.

'I AM' is like the old swinging door in the western movies.

No weakness implied, just flexibility to the choice made by the individual. This is how spiritual law works. It has the power to create and destroy. It is like electricity. Electricity will cook the man's food, but it will also cook the man if he violates the law. This is because whatever you say after 'I AM' becomes your reality, prosperity or poverty. Let's stay on the positive side of 'I AM'. *It is the door to the treasure house of abundant life, the life of prosperity. To experience abundance and prosperity start affirming 'I AM Prospering' now! When you do this, you will find the door and go in and out and find food. You should constantly affirm; 'I AM abundantly supplied!'*

The Master-Teacher and Central Figure of the Gospels said; "I am come that ye might have Life and that ye might have it more abundantly" **(John 10:10)**. Notice: 'I AM come that you might have life!'

I AM COME... I AM HAS COME!!!

The Great I AM came in the person of Jesus Christ to give you access ^(an opened door) to abundant life. This abundant life is manifested for you by affirming 'I AM! I AM is the *Way*, I AM is the *Truth* and I AM is the *LIFE*. *How do you tap-in to that life?* It is simple; you tap in by blending with this *LIFE* and by affirming 'I AM'. More so, you do it by the spoken word. Your affirmation makes your world that of prosperity by opening the *Door* of abundance. This '*Door* of I AM' will bring you into the House of Abundance where you can feast.

ONE WITH CHRIST - THE ONE

You mature as you learn to live in awareness of being one with the *Great I Am, the One, the Christ*. You can then boldly affirm with *Him*; I AM! You can only affirm this after getting the revelation of the awareness of *being* one with the *Great I AM*.

Affirm throughout today that 'I AM one with Christ, the One'. Continue to live in that mental atmosphere all day; then you will draw out the Wisdom, Power, and Infinite Intelligence within you. Christ is in you.

Your *entire* world will be transformed by the affirmation of 'I AM' one with Christ. Every time you say; 'I AM' one with Christ, you affirmatively submerge your consciousness with Christ. You are praying affirmatively. Affirmative prayer programs the human consciousness with power. It also opens the *Door* to be blessed. Being blessed means empowered to prosper. I AM is Christ in you, the Hope or confident expectation of prosperity. So where does God live? Do you know His address...?

AFFIRM:

"I AM lives within me, I am one with Him!"

'I AM' JOURNAL

_____

_____

_____

_____

_____

_____

_____

_____

_____

_____

_____

_____

_____

_____

_____

_____

_____

_____

_____

_____

CHAPTER 8
GOD'S ADDRESS

"I am one with the abundance within me."

WHAT IS GOD'S ADDRESS, HIS LOCATION? *Have you ever thought about this?* As long as you believe in a God that is in the far away starry heavens, you will continue to transfer the power of your manifestation away, forgetting that you are the conceiver. *What do you mean Bernard?* I mean; you are the one who must exercise faith to see your desires come to pass.

Now get this; *YOU ARE THE OPERANT POWER!*

You are the conceiver!

Conception with relation to childbirth is the time when sperm travels up through the vagina and fertilizes an egg found in the fallopian tube. **In simple terms, it is to get pregnant.** Conceive, according to the Thesaurus Dictionary means; to imagine, visualize, envision, create, consider. Remember that to *visualize* is a part of VAM.

You can and *MUST* conceive and believe to achieve. To manifest, you must conceive. **I repeat! You are the conceiver!** Say "I am the conceiver!"

GOD'S ADDRESS IS 'I AM'!

You will start conceiving and giving birth once you discover God's address. You must know the power of 'I AM' *within* you, and not in some far away heaven.

So, *what is God's address?* It is within you. The Great 'I AM' is definitely within you. The Word is near you, even in your mouth and in your heart.

God is the Word!

God is I AM!

God's address is within, even in your mouth.

God's address is I AM!

Abundance is in your mouth and heart. You must say 'I AM prosperous' in order to activate the prosperity within you.

DO YOU BELIEVE?

Jesus Christ the master teacher asked; "Do you believe that *I AM* is able to do this?" Notice the phrase 'I AM'. You could say *He* was asking; *DO YOU BELIEVE THAT THE 'I AM' IS ABLE TO DO THIS?* If you believe in 'I AM', then claim yourself to *be* that which you want and see it manifested in your life. Claim yourself to be that prosperity which you want and that you shall be. Be prosperous within by putting the affirmations of prosperity in your mouth and you will manifest prosperity in your world.

I AM PROSPERITY

We increase or limit our prosperity by the way we identify ourselves. Most people identify themselves negatively as weak, defeated, and even poor. This negative self-identification can be subtle such as: *"I AM only a poor person."* Change your conception of yourself and you will, without the aid of anyone else, automatically transform your world to conform to your changed conception of yourself. Identify yourself with prosperity by saying;

"I AM PROSPERITY!"

"I AM PROSPERITY!"

"I AM PROSPERITY!"

Be aware of what you tie your "I AM" to. This is a powerful act of calling the creative process into flow. There is but *One Way, One Truth, One Life, One Intelligence, One I AM, One Presence*, and this is the fact, that 'I AM' lives in you.

You are identified with 'I AM'!

You are one with *Him*!

You are one with prosperity!

WITHIN IS POWER TO WIN

'I AM' is the fact of your existence.

To know 'I AM' gives you all the power you need to win. When you have to go out into the world and tackle the proverbial *'Egyptians'* or enemies and your heart turns to water within you, and you say to yourself; "I cannot do this, I am not adequate or there is no way" Always remember your true identity and say to the *'Egyptians'* enemies, "*I AM HATH SENT ME!!*" When you do, the road will open and you will conquer your difficulties. Before you can be able to transform your world from debt to abundance, you must first lay the foundation or understanding of the concept of 'I AM'. You must know God's address. Affirm: *'I AM is NOW WITHIN!' WITHIN IS THE POWER TO WIN!!!*

AFFIRM:

"I AM one with the Great 'I AM'! I AM is within!"

'I AM' JOURNAL

CHAPTER 9

SHOOT FOR THE MOON

"I am a possibility thinker."

Are you a *possibility thinker?* You have heard the expression: "Oh, he is reaching for the moon again!" It could be a pessimistic friend or relative speaking of an ambition, based upon your desire or dream. You may want to transcend *(which means to rise above)* the limitation of your world of poverty, lack, and debt. Perhaps, this is the mentality and environment in which you were born and raised. Or it could be some personal financial ambition to do something extraordinary, and people who know your natural limitations will say things about you like; "Oh! Here we go again, he is reaching for the moon". Your intention could be the desire to be great, rich or even famous, as many have done throughout history. The *Great I AM* promised to make Abraham famous.

Abraham and his seed were reaching to conquer the earth, metaphorically reaching for the moon. Through the power of 'I AM', all things are possible with you. You can shoot for the moon.

FAITH SHOOTS FOR THE MOON

Now, let's make *living and moving in faith* practical. Practical entails practicing it. I am here to teach you spiritual practices. Living in practical faith involves the use of the human imagination, which is the key to power. We have greatly neglected the power of the human imagination.

God said of the people when they attempted to build the tower to heaven; "nothing shall be restrained from them which they have imagined to do." That means all things are possible to the human imagination. This is where VAM comes in.

If you could get into your imaginative faith-based images, approach and dwell in them on the basis of your meditative positive thought, you would realize that all things are possible to him who believes. You would realize faith and become a possibility thinker. The process of Visualization, Affirmation, and Meditation (VAM) realizes this practical faith. You get into it and then it gets into you!

When you visualize and imagine the end result over time, you will have a clear image of what you desire. You have faith which is the substance of the things you hope for.

You affirm your faith by speaking to the mountain, and then you meditate upon the *Word* and your desire being a reality. You perceive as real fact that which is not revealed to the senses.

If I would realize faith in spite of the limitations that now surround me such as lack of money, lack of time and present obligations, I would manifest my desire. *I MUST ENTER INTO THE IMAGE*, regardless of what I see or feel.

In the beginning, it may be difficult. But you can achieve it with practice. You must VAM *(Visualize, Affirm and Meditate)* on the prosperity and success you desire. Standing even in the face of lack, debt and limitation, you must shut out all unbelief and enter the image by faith.

You must imagine the desired end!

You must live in the end!

The reason you must do this is practical and simple: **"Energy flows where attention goes!"**

Put your attention on your desire and the energy of faith will flow there. You must shut out all unbelief and enter the image and vision by faith. *How?* You imagine it being done by faith. *Have you ever done this?*

As you get into the state of your desire and dwell there, *(continue therein)* you will manifest it. **Believe that you have received and you shall have it.**

Everything you see now was first imagined. The things that are seen were not made of things which do appear. Everything was made from the invisible or *Divine Power of Imagination.* When you VAM *(Visualize, Affirm and Meditate)*, you engage your imagination. This is Divine Power of Imagination. Imagining is what we name this power.

Imagining is the greatest spiritual secret in the world. Imagination is possibility thinking, shooting for the moon!

AFFIRM:

I become what I imagine myself to be!

'I AM' JOURNAL

_____

_____

_____

_____

_____

_____

_____

_____

_____

_____

_____

_____

_____

_____

_____

_____

_____

CHAPTER 10

IMAGINATION + FAITH

"I am living in the overflow of prosperity by imaginative faith."

A nyone who finds spiritual insight into imagination, finds the key to abundant life. Everyone should seek after this Divine Secret of Imagination. I will endeavor to make this as plain as possible for you. God the *Great I AM* lives within you as we have seen. Scripture teaches that God dwells in your heart by your faith *(consider this for a moment)*. You could say; *'I AM dwells in your faith and God dwells in your affirmation of I AM.'* All things are possible to God and if you can believe all things are possible to you. All things are possible to you because God the *Great I AM*, dwells in your faith. Faith is simply *'I AM consciousness.'* You are a God-IAM indwelt being. His address is within you. Your belief in this increases your consciousness of *His* Presence.

Spend a moment meditating on the *Great I AM* dwelling in your heart by faith. Imagine it!

IMAGINATION + FAITH

How does imagination and faith work together?

Here is a statement to meditate on; *"What is now true was once only imagined."* The *Great I AM* creates through the human imagination on earth. Here is why; Imagination works with faith, in the invisible realm. The principle of faith is *'things that are seen were made by the unseen'.* For example; let's say you are in a room. It seems so real. Well, this room was once only imagined. The room, along with the facility or house came out of the imagination of someone. Someone conceived it, believed it and achieved it!

OUT-PICTURED IMAGINATION

Here is another example; you are wearing dresses, suits, and all kinds of outfits, but they had to be imagined first. The outfit started in the invisible world and was out-pictured, or manifested. To out-picture is to manifest something from within. If you have ever used a tailor, you know the process. As a professional musician, I certainly have. Here is how it works. You go to a tailor or your dressmaker and you pick out the material that you like. It's just a plain piece of cloth. Then you tell your dressmaker or tailor what kind of outfit or dress you want. So you allow him with his or her talent, to make your vision or imagined garment come into a reality of the kind of a suit or dress that you want. He executes it or out-pictures it.

He started with just a picture and then manifested what you imagined. *Now what is the outfit?* **It is the manifestation of imagination.** It is an out-picturing of an image you had within. This must be understood! Remember that it was first only imagined. Everything works that way. Imagination is a function of faith.

IMAGINATION + FAITH = Manifestation!

IMAGINE WEALTH

Wealth starts with the imagination, unless you were born rich. For example, a poor or a man of moderate means imagines wealth. When he becomes wealthy, he may forget the means by which it came about and thinks only about the external forces that were used to bring it to pass. The power to create wealth started from imagination, which is the cause of his wealth and not the external forces. They had to play their various parts as he imagined what he imagined.

When one imagines wealth and adds 'I AM' wealth affirmations to his inner conversation, Imagination plus faith produces wealth. This is how wealth is transferred to the man of imagination. You must first of all see it within.

Remember Abraham? He saw it in imagination before his blessing manifested.

...Lift up now your eyes, and look ***from the place*** where you are, northward, and southward, and eastward, and westward: For all the land which you see [imagine], to you will I give it, and to your seed forever.

Genesis 13:14-15 *(Paraphrased)*

The *Great I AM* told Abraham to lift up his imaginative eyes from the place he stood in and imagine the land he would inherit first, and then *He* eventually made Abraham rich. Actually, Abraham's imagination made him rich. He imagined the vision of wealth and greatness.

He Visualized! He Affirmed! He meditated! VAM!!

That's why he is the father of biblical faith.

What about you? How do you manifest?

You Imagine 'I AM'. Identify yourself with 'I AM' now! This will determine the circumstances of your life. In this journey of self-discovery, do not allow anything to interfere with your discovery of 'I AM'.

Affirm: *'I AM a God inside minded being! I AM a God indwelt being. All things are possible by Him and He dwells in me. So I realize that all things are possible with me. I engage in I AM imagination.'*

Who am I?

I am who I imagine myself to be. I AM THAT!!!

AFFIRM:

"I AM prosperous because I imagine prosperity.
I AM!"

'I AM' JOURNAL

_____

_____

_____

_____

_____

_____

_____

_____

_____

_____

_____

_____

_____

_____

_____

_____

_____

_____

_____

_____

CHAPTER 11
IMAGINATION IS SOWING

"I am sowing thoughts of prosperity and attracting money easily."

H ave you ever asked yourself; *what am I imagining?* If you haven't, do it now! We all imagine. The only difference is with what we imagine; the content of our imaginations. That is an amazing fact; we all imagine. What I imagine always eventually becomes reality in my life. This is because what I imagine becomes my inner-conversation or my 'I AM'.

Everything that manifests in your life including your wealth, works through your imagination which is the power to create wealth. This is how it works:

1) You *imagine or sow* it!

2) You *visualize* it!

3) You *affirm* it or say it!

4) You *meditate* on it!

5) Then you *manifest* it!

The choice is always yours. You are at the helm. Imagination puts you in the driver's seat.

You are what you imagine.

You reap what you sow!

You can imagine poverty or prosperity, sickness or health. The choice is yours. But remember, when you make the choice, the choice controls the chooser.

The choice you make is what you sow and manifest. What you choose to imagine is what you out-picture. As such, prosperity is yours for the choosing. If I choose to imagine poverty and feel sorry for myself, life will prove that I had every reason in the world to feel sorry for myself, because the bad breaks will come to me.

It's actually up to us to imagine the abundance, which could have attracted good breaks and great opportunities. We often turn to blame circumstances or people for bad results, when ultimately the blame is on our very selves. Have you ever done this? I have.

The truth is, if I did not have such imaginations, I would not have encountered the conditions I manifested.

You become what you imagine!

You become what you think about.

This is the Law! This may seem hard and harsh, but it is really liberation. You are at the helm. The choice is yours.

The reason this works is the basic law of cause and effect or what the Bible calls sowing and reaping.

IMAGINATION IS SOWING

We are told in scripture: "Don't fool yourself. God is not mocked! This is spiritual law. As a man sows, so shall he reap" **(Galatians 6:7)**. Well, the big question is *what am I sowing?* I am sowing everything that I am imagining. Imagination is sowing.

That is what I am sowing, for the only thing I can *'sow'* is what I imagine. **Life is imagination in manifestation.**

How is this true? What you sow or imagine is what you reap or harvest.

Imagination is your life because it is causation. Wow! *Wonder of wonders.* Imagination creates or causes reality, and it has the power to create wealth. Moreover, it is spiritual law because you become what you imagine.

It has been said that the number one quality of the billionaire is his imagination.

Imagination is the key to wealth. Imagine wealth, prosperity, possibility, and even billions. *Do you want billions?* It is possible. For with God, all things are possible and to him who believes.

AFFIRM:

"I AM imagining and attracting money easily and effortlessly."

'I AM' JOURNAL

CHAPTER 12
THE ART OF BELIEVING!

"I am increasingly magnetic to wealth, abundance, prosperity, and money."

A great question for you coming up. *Is there an art in believing?* If yes, *what is it?* This is the answer I found. With no room in my imagination for doubt, I will be in the process of learning the art of believing. Imagination is the key. **Stop imagining doubt and start learning how to believe, even when your five physical senses and reason denies it. I believe even when my senses try to prevent me from believing.** Faith perceives as real fact that which is not revealed to the five physical senses. It also creates a capacity for God to fit into our lives.

Faith works largely through our imagination.

Faith imagines the desired result. We must choose to believe. We imagine that we have received, and we shall have. Knowing is one thing and believing is another.

Apply faith and you will know it and realize it.

We were created to live by faith.

"We are led to believe a lie when we see with and not through the eyes." –Blake

MENTAL JOURNEYS

The inner body of man is the imagination. Once you realize and grasp this insight, you will start to embark on mental journeys. Many spiritual people frown on teachings about the imagination and the mind, but it is vital to have a good understanding of the importance of these mental journeys. A mental journey is the practice or exercise of bi-location. **Bilocation** sometimes called multi-location, is where an individual or object is located ^(or appears to be located) in two distinct places at the same time. The Apostle Paul said; *"though I am absent in body, I am with you in spirit."* This is a biblical reference to bilocation. *How can one be in two places at one time?* In imagination! It puts you where you picture yourself to be. You can imagine yourself as rich even while in the space of poverty.

INNER MOVEMENT

This concept is a lot more powerful than most people have imagined. Imagination is inner movement, which produces corresponding outer movements off money and goods. All movement is from within. The Apostle Paul through prayer, meditation, and imagination from within, pictured himself to be at a different location in spirit. This is a spiritual practice of faith. Faith is inner movement or active spiritual energy.

Faith sees or imagines things that are not as though they were. For example The *Great I AM* told Joshua; "every place that the sole of your foot shall tread I have given you."

The first exercise of faith is always inner movement by imagination.

IMAGINE JERICHO

Joshua had to imagine having Jericho before it manifested. Scripture says; "See I have given you Jericho..." **(Joshua 6:1-3)**. Faith is an inner action. Inner action is a concept called introverted sensation. *What do we mean here?* You construct a scene from within you through faith and imagination before you can see it in the material world. This is the creative principle. *(we will discuss this later in the creative process)*.

Imagination creates reality.

Imagination creates wealth. This is why a person's state of mind is the state of his prosperity.

The great Emerson said; "What we are, that only can we see."

Your outer world is only actualized inner-movement. That is a statement worthy of meditation. ***Your outer world is only actualized inner-movement.***

As a man thinks within, so is he. He must be fully persuaded in his own mind. Your inner conversation will always match your fulfilled desire. When you imagine something strongly within, it is eventually manifested. What you desire to hear without, you must hear within. The battle is in one's own imagination. This is the good fight of faith. It is always within first!

"We are led to believe a lie when we see with and not through the eyes." –Blake

INNER TALKING

Your inner talking is the key to your imagination and your prosperity. *Why Bernard?* Because what you are saying within, you are imagining. *What are you saying within?*

What are you imagining within, poverty or prosperity? The choice is yours. This is why affirmation is so important and powerful. Our outer affirmation mirrors our 'inner talking' or imagination. This is huge!

Just think now, you always imagine what you are saying to yourself. You always imagine your inner talking. Here is a simple example. Say the word *dog* to yourself five times. If you say to yourself *dog, what do you imagine?* You imagine a dog, and not a cow. If you say big hairy brown dog, *what do you imagine?* A big hairy brown dog!!!

What's the point here? Imagination mirrors inner talking or the state with which it is fused. Spirituality is all about inner-working. Go to work on your with-in-ness.

To change the state, we must change our inner talking. VAM is designed to change your inner talking. As you visualize the desired result, affirm what you want and meditate on the objective and intention. By this, you will change your inner talking. This (VAM) is a spiritual practice that exercises and trains your inner world.

The key is to 'identify within' with your aim. As a man thinks in his heart, so is he. The creation of wealth starts from within. This process requires patience. Many miss it here. They are impatient. It takes faith and patience to inherit the promises.

The reason it takes patience becomes simple the moment you understand how things manifest. **All things are created twice; first within, then on the outside.** The principle is *faith* first, *manifestation* second. This is why without faith, it is impossible to please 'I AM'. *He* is pleased and has pleasure in our prosperity which is always created twice by faith. Prosperity consciousness within will always manifests or out-pictures prosperity without. Faith prospers us from the inside out. It is not about the money and stuff. It is inside out. It is all within first. Prosperity from within produces wealth without...

Does this make sense?

MATURE FAITH

In the early stages of faith, every goal$^{(objective)}$ and venture will seem to be about you being successful with material things. As an immature believer you think that you are primarily here to increase your income and have the things of this world that you so desire. But after a while, you will mature in faith and realize that material things are only toys to amuse you until the maturity of faith is realized. Then, you will know that you are not just here to amass a fortune, but to make a difference in society.

AFFIRM:

"I AM increasingly magnetic to wealth, abundance, prosperity, and money."

'I AM' JOURNAL

_____
_____
_____
_____
_____
_____
_____
_____
_____
_____
_____
_____
_____
_____
_____
_____
_____
_____
_____
_____
_____

CHAPTER 13
PROSPERITY WITHIN

"I am attracting more and more abundance

into my life every day."

N ow that you are grasping the concept of I AM, I want to ask you some empowering questions.

What is your grand intention in life?

What is the dream that you have?

What is the BIG thing?

What is your life goal?

What is your mission in life? Is it just to get rich with material things? Contrary to popular belief, I am not promoting materialism in this book. *Why?* My teaching is that, wealth is within. The inner world is the source of true wealth. Once we are really spiritually awakened, we will realize that our interests lie mostly in the inner world. This is because the physical world is not the reality but the inner world. Once awakened to the secret of 'I AM consciousness', we no longer find the need to accumulate unnecessary physical objects. When you do, prosperity will flow like a river. As you stay awakened, you tame the anxiety and cares of this world in your life. **You transcend it!** As you transcend the material world, you realize that all things are yours. How do you transcend the world?

You rise above the materialistic point of view.

You stop the fight for wealth.

You become a giver.

You become a liberal soul.

As a liberal soul you will be made prosperous.

The liberal soul is a prosperous soul. Giving opens the door to wealth in your life. Giving is receiving. Giving and receiving is a spiritual circle or cycle. Selah.

Scripture teaches that a generous soul will prosper, and he who refreshes others will himself be refreshed.

I AM CONSCIOUSNESS

This is a suggestion that will serve you well. Do not fight against financial conditions. *Why?* They only reflect the chaos within you. Turn your back on the outward material world and pay attention WITHIN, as you would physically turn your back upon that which you do not want to see as you turn to that which you want to see. *How?*

Develop a proper prosperity consciousness. Make this 'I AM' consciousness your new self-concept.

What are we saying? We are basically saying that our sense of 'I AM' consciousness in life is the one thing that transcends the physical self and links us to the inner spiritual self. When we hold onto this sense of 'I AM', it will always lead us to the abundant Life without failure. Attention must be turned from the outward world back to the inward world. The kingdom is within you. *IT IS WITHIN,* which eventually becomes our mantra. Your daily VAM workshop is designed to develop you within.

SPIRITUAL EXERCISE

I have found that most people are not familiar with spiritual practices such as meditation. They just don't know how to do it. So, here is a simple spiritual exercise. I will walk you through it. First just **relax.** Release all tension from your shoulders. Release all stress in your mind. Breathe in deeply through your nostrils and breathe out slowly through your mouth. Repeat this breathing exercise three to five times. Now close your eyes and silently feel and affirm over and over to yourself; '*I Am, I Am, I Am That, I Am That...*' Don't condition it, just affirm I am! As you affirm 'I AM', you release the inner man, the spiritual man. You simply affirm '*I Am That.... I Am.*'

Do you sense more peace within now?

This simple practice will produce an expansion of consciousness if repeated daily. Practice this during your VAM workshop for thirty days. The expanded prosperity consciousness will automatically manifest increased prosperity. This is because whatever you have in consciousness manifests in life. As the ancients taught; *LIFE IS CONSCIOUSNESS.* As consciousness expands, awareness expands. This expanded awareness is the proper way to true and lasting prosper. This is prosperity or wealth from the inside out. The world teaches you how to prosper from the outside in. The world teaches you how to grind and toil. Grinding and toiling is not your portion because this toiling is not *Divine prosperity.* Prosperity consciousness produces prosperity by Divine Right. 'I AM' gives you proper prosperity or sweat-less prosperity. The blessing of the *LORD* makes you rich and adds no sorrow or toiling with it. This is prosperity from the inside out. You will grow larger inwardly. You become bigger on the inside. You then become financially and bigger on the outside. Expansion within manifests expansion without.

When an expansion of consciousness is attained, you will become a big giver of your finances and resources, and move into new manifestations of prosperity. This is what happened with the early Christians in the book of Acts of the Apostles. They eradicated, wiped out poverty, debt and lack in the whole church.

'Nor was there anyone among them who lacked; for all who were possessors of lands or houses sold them, and brought the proceeds of the things that were sold...'

--Acts 4: 34 (NKJV)

Developing the 'I AM' consciousness will bring change to the entire community. It will bring change to your concept of yourself and that will bring an increase of prosperity into your life.

As you now discover that *'deep'* within yourself, all things are yours. Anything you can conceive of being will seem to be. This is the true realm of faith.

This is what the early believers had because they had been taught and trained how to manifest wealth without toil. Jesus constantly taught this. What are we teaching today?

MOVING DEEPER

In order to catch that which is beyond your present consciousness, you must dive down deeper waters. You must launch out into the deep.

Going deeper is not complicated. It simply requires taking your attention away from the material world. Take your attention away from your present problem or limitations and dwell upon just being 'I AM'.

Say to yourself over and over again, *'I AM, I AM, I AM!'*

Persist until you cut the anchor that binds you to your problems and you will move out into the depth of their solution. This is the *TRUE* abundant life Jesus Christ promised. This is living in 'I AM' Intention.

AFFIRM:

"I AM attracting more and more abundance into my life every day."

'I AM' JOURNAL

_____
_____
_____
_____
_____
_____
_____
_____
_____
_____
_____
_____
_____
_____
_____
_____
_____
_____
_____
_____

CHAPTER 14

THE LAW OF ATTRACTION

"I am attracting abundance."

S o, what is a spiritual law? It is a process that always works. It works every time we put it to test. Like the law of gravity, spiritual law is consistent and works all the time. It is no respecter of persons. I find that so intriguing. Abundance is impartial. It works by law. The Law of attraction is one such law. *Have you ever studied 'The Law of Attraction'?* I personally think it is basic knowledge everyone on earth should have. It is so powerful. It is a prevailing law that states; *'THAT WHICH IS LIKE UNTO ITSELF IS DRAWN.'* This is why it is called the Law of Attraction. It attracts! This law is closely related to the *Law of 'I AM'*. How? Stated in its most basic form, the Law of 'I AM' states that; *WHATEVER YOU SAY AFTER 'I AM' IS CREATED IN YOUR LIFE.* The law of 'I AM' goes hand in hand with the Law of Attraction. The Law of Attraction primarily involves *THOUGHTS* while the Law of 'I AM' involves *WORDS*. Thoughts and words work together because a thought is an unspoken word, while a word is simply a spoken thought. *Are we connecting the dots now?*

LOA*(law of attraction)* says, 'whatever you think about, talk about, believe strongly about and feel intensely about, you will *BRING ABOUT* in your life'. In essence, 'thoughts are things!' This is brought out clearly in Napoleon Hill's classic book, 'Think and Grow Rich.' THOUGHTS ARE THINGS!!

THOUGHTS & WORDS RULE

The great Jack Canfield has said; *"In the real sense, our thoughts and words have power over our lives. And as such, it's a good idea to be intentional about the thoughts and words you put out there. If you have specific life or career or financial goals, for instance, why not focus your thoughts on achieving those goals and having that good come into your life. Why not see, think about and affirm the desired end?"* That's the law of attraction. That's what faith does. That is the Power of 'I AM'.

You affirm the desired goal as already done *now*!

Now I want to share a formula with you that will activate and get the Law of Attraction working effectively in your life.

This formula was discussed in *'The Secret'* as the Creative Process. By the way, Rhonda Byrne the author of *'The Secret'* even said that this was taken directly from the Bible. It is amazing how much the Bible was quoted or referred to in the program. The 'I AM' Principles are universal. They work for all who put them to work. Here is The Creative Process.

The ASK – BELIEVE – RECEIVE formula:

Ask - Believe - Receive

Ask

> *'Ask, and it shall be given you; seek, and ye shall find; knock, and it shall be opened unto you'.* **Matthew 7:7**

Let's begin with 'asking'. The key is to focus on and ask for what you want versus what you don't want. So, you must start being intentional while regarding what you think and talk about all day.

Are you immersing yourself in positive, uplifting, joyful thoughts? Do you <u>meditate</u> and hold pictures of what you want in your life in your mind? Or do you frequently criticize yourself and others, complain about your life and focus on your lack of abundance?

Feeling excited, enthusiastic, passionate, happy, joyful, loving, appreciative, prosperous and peaceful are thoughts and feelings that give off positive energy. You should intentionally start creating your future in your mind, and then ask for what you want while ignoring what you don't want. Continually affirm 'I AM THAT' to manifest what you have asked for. Affirming 'I AM' will cause the people, situations, money, resources, and opportunities necessary to bring about what you have asked for.

Believe

'And all things, whatsoever ye shall ask in prayer, believing, ye shall receive'. **Matthew 21:22**

The next step is to believe. *What does it mean to ask and believe for what you want?* It means maintaining a positive expectancy, going about your day with certainty, knowing that you have put your future in the hands of the *Great I AM*...and that *He* will deliver. **Always act as if what you want is on its way.** It is simply a matter of you deciding with conviction that what you want and asked for is yours. Many people have limiting beliefs that keep them from allowing abundance and happiness into their lives. If this describes you, realize that you must first change your limiting beliefs into thoughts that you deserve and are worthy of abundance. Believe that 'I AM' is *the One* who is more than enough for you in every way. Only Believe.

Take Action!

Once you believe, taking the corresponding actions that would create your desired result affirms your belief that what you want is within reach. After all, you would not be taking action if you did not expect your future situation to manifest, *would you?* So, taking action is a demonstration of your belief. Faith without corresponding actions is dead.

Receive

> *'Therefore I say unto you, what things soever ye desire, when ye pray, believe that ye receive them, and ye shall have them'.* **Mark 11:24**

The final step of this creative process is to believe you receive what you want by faith. You do this by becoming a vibrational match for it. *What do you mean by a vibrational match? Don't get spooky Bernard!* I won't. I realize that there is mega ignorance of the law of vibration. So let me explain; everyone on the planet is like a radio station that is broadcasting on a specific frequency. If you want to listen to jazz, you have to tune your dial to a station that broadcasts jazz, not one that plays hip-hop or country. Likewise, if you want more abundance and prosperity in your life, you have to tune the frequency of your thoughts and attention to ones of abundance and prosperity. After tuning in, you must affirm abundance. This is where you use the 'I AM' affirmations in your VAM workshop at the back of this book. If you follow this process, you will attract more abundance into your life. That is how you harness the power of 'I AM'.

Now, let's explain the "Law of Vibration." When we have thoughts, we send out vibrations. This is not religion folks it science. A thought has a vibratory force, and these vibrations are of such a fine, ethereal substance that the natural senses such as the ear cannot pick up on it. Now, I believe when you have a spiritual ear, you can pick up on people's thoughts. *'Bernard, what are you talking about?'* Well, the Bible says that Jesus Christ knew their thoughts. Now wait, this is not as far out as you think. He knew their thoughts because he picked up on the vibratory energy, or force, of those thoughts. These vibrations are not evident to our five senses, so it seems to us that there is no proof of their existence. Most people say; "if I can't see, feel, touch, smell or taste it, then it doesn't exist."

Well, let's illustrate this by considering a magnet. Thought is just like a powerful magnet that sends out vibrations and exerts a force so dominant that it draws steel to it. *Do you see the force of the magnet? Do you see the drawing power?* No, you don't see it. But this magnet can attract a piece of steel weighing 100 pounds if it's a big and powerful enough magnet. We can neither see, taste, smell, hear nor feel the mighty force of the magnet. These thought vibrations likewise cannot be seen, tasted, neither smelled or heard, nor felt in any other way. But they work by spiritual law.

Light and heat are manifestations of vibration, of a far lower intensity than even thought, but the difference is solely the rate of vibration. Now, even light and heat are a result of vibration. Everything in this universe works by the law of vibration. The law of attraction and the law of vibration work together. Prayer is the law of vibration in action. Keep reading!

You are doing great.

Next, let's consider a little closer look at the law of being...

AFFIRM:

I AM attracting abundance now!

'I AM' JOURNAL

_____

_____

_____

_____

_____

_____

_____

_____

_____

_____

_____

_____

_____

_____

_____

_____

_____

_____

_____

_____

_____

CHAPTER 15

THE LAW OF BEING LORD!

"I am radiating abundance."

N ow that we have basically covered the concept of 'I AM', let us move in a little more closer and deeper and gain some further insight into the *Law of BEING*. Insight literally means sight-within. So, we are expanding our intrinsic understanding of the Law of BEING. Understand that the first time you hear a truth brings awareness. Deeper insight brings expanded awareness. We now know that 'I AM' is the law of your being which is the foundation of your very existence.

LORD/LAW

One of the greatest understandings to gain in our growth is that the word *LORD* is often interchangeable in meaning with LAW. Consequently, the LAW of your being could be understood as the *LORD* of your being. Open your mind to the insight here.

'I am the LORD, and there is no other besides me. There is no God; I equip you, though you do not know me...'

Isaiah 45: 5 (ESV)

Now, here is the insight: *I am the LORD*, and *there is no other*, could have been translated 'I AM' is the LAW. Here's why; The LAW equips us with understanding.

'I AM is the LAW' in your life because your 'I AM' *lords* it over your entire life. *Why?* When you say 'I AM', that is the force that shapes your life. *YOU BECOME ONE WITH YOUR 'I AM!'* This is true because 'I AM' is the Divine Nature within. If you find that difficult to grasp, just remember the power of your words. You can have what you say is a spiritual law. Your words dominate or lord it over your life.

BEING!

Every time you say 'I AM', you release *BEING.*

This is because 'I AM' is the LORD of BEING! It is the Law of BEING. 'I AM' spoken by your lips is a result of your awareness of being. To make it practical, you always eventually manifest that which you are aware of being.

'I AM' is continually BEING!

FENTON'S MODERN LORD'S PRAYER

To help you understand the Law of BEING, I will share Ferrar Fenton's translation of *The Lord's Prayer*, which is found in 'The Complete Bible in Modern English' published in 1903. The Fenton Bible was one of the earliest translations of the Bible into modern English. Fenton drives home the truth of the law of BEING.

Mr. Fenton said regarding his version of the Lord's Prayer; "This is a literal translation of the original Greek, retaining the Greek moods and tenses by the clearest English I could.

The old versions, having been made from a Latin translation, could not reproduce the actual sense of the *Savior* as given by the evangelists for Latin has no Aorist*(tense)* of the imperative passive mood used by Matthew and Luke. The force of the imperative first Aorist*(tense)* seems to me to be that of what is called **a standing order**, a thing to **be done absolutely**, and continuously."

Notice that according to Fenton's interpretation of the Aorist tense, the Lord's Prayer is not a prayer for something to be done in the future, but rather our recognition that God is continually manifesting these things in the present. Now!

This is a prayer of the NOW!

This prayer is a prayer of affirmations!

This is a prayer of continuous BEING!

THE PRAYER

"For your Father knows your necessities before you ask Him. Consequently, you must pray in this way: *Our Father in the Heavens; Your Name* **must be being** *Hallowed; Your Kingdom* **must be being** *restored. Your Will* **must be being done** *both in Heaven and upon the Earth. Give us today our tomorrow's bread; And forgive us our faults, as we forgive those offending us, for You would not lead us into temptation, but deliver us from its evil.*"

Jesus said pray; Your Name must BE BEING hallowed NOW, Your kingdom must BE BEING restored NOW, Your will must BE BEING done NOW! *Why now?* This is because we are dealing with 'I AM', *which is BEING* now. Faith is always now!!

Now, faith is the substance of things hoped for the evidence of things not seen. **(Hebrews 11:1)**

FAITH IS ALWAYS NOW! BEING IS ALWAYS NOW! This is a prayer of calling things into BEING NOW! Prosperity is NOW!

Save now, I pray, O LORD; O LORD, I pray, send now prosperity. **(Psalm 118:25)**

Notice the *He said; 'send NOW' prosperity*. That is the now faith principle. Faith calls things that *be* not as though they were. Faith calls things into being NOW. That is the essence of 'I AM'. The 'I AM' affirmations create wealth because of the law of faith.

Affirm out loud: *'I AM PROSPERITY NOW! I AM!'*

We are gaining insight into the law of faith. Faith is always now, so saying 'I AM PROSPERITY' is affirming that I am BEING prosperity NOW by faith. *Do you get it?* I am not trying to obtain prosperity. 'I AM BEING PROSPERITY NOW.' Remember Fenton's emphasis on the phrase 'Be BEING' in the Modern Translation of the Prayer!

Jesus taught the power of BEING. *He* taught this continuously, but most religious people missed it because they were blinded by tradition. Jesus taught us to make declarations and affirmations in the NOW. He taught affirmative prayer. The Lord's Prayer which many of us learned way back in the day is an Affirmative prayer. Wow! I find this most interesting and exciting!

NO LACK IN THE UNIVERSE

In the light of NOW PROSPERITY, realize that 'There is no lack in the universe.' Lack is a mental creation that defies the wholeness of the universe. Lack is made possible by the freedom of man to apply his mind to any objective of his choice and become subjected to it. By Divine design there is no lack. Conditions of lack are reflections of the negative mind. This is simply wrong thinking. Lack was created by the thoughts of man. Difficulties, struggles, and unbalanced pain are the manifestations of wrong thinking or a mind in a mental wilderness. Spiritual Law always grants exemptions to the *will* of man thereby allowing the mind to be a law unto itself, even if the law is a manifestation of foolishness. Simply said 'I AM' ***will manifest whatever you choose to affirm as your reality, even lack.*** Yet, there is no lack in God's way of doing things. You can choose to believe in lack by saying; '*I AM poor*'. Your 'I AM' becomes your reality. This happened to Adam and Eve. They chose a belief in lack while in the Garden of Eden which was a place of abundance.

YOU ARE PROSPERITY!

You cannot be in lack if you believe that you BE-BEING prosperity. Say it again: *I AM PROSPERITY NOW!* Say it ten or twenty times until you are comfortable with it; '*I AM PROSPERITY NOW!*' Affirming this develops in you a prosperity consciousness.

BUT I AM IN LACK

You say, how can you say there is no lack when I am in lack? Well, notice you said *'I AM in lack!'* If you are in lack, it means you are violating the unity of the universe by engaging in wrong thinking. All negative manifestations in life stem from our wrong thinking. The chaos resulting in the law of vibration from 'wrong thinking' is manifesting as lack. Right thinking is prosperous thinking. To live in prosperity, right thinking has to be the first principle in your mind. This is simply spiritual law. Everything starts with 'I AM'!

So, what do I need to do Bernie? Believe!

It's not something you have to force yourself to believe. It is a fact to calmly accept, 'I AM PROSPERITY'. Just let this 'I AM' consciousness settle into your spirit as you relax and wonder at the marvels of the universe, the goodness of God. **There is no lack in the universe!**

AFFIRM:

I AM blessed with all-sufficiency!

'I AM' JOURNAL

_____
_____
_____
_____
_____
_____
_____
_____
_____
_____
_____
_____
_____
_____
_____
_____
_____
_____

CHAPTER 16

'I AM' THE NAME OF GOD

"I am flowing in the abundance of I AM."

We have come to the final chapter in our I AM journey. You have made it and stayed with it to the end. Congratulations! I commend you for being a real truth student. We have saved the best for last. Let's wrap this book up by learning the benefits of knowing *God's* name.

Who is the Being we call God? How do you identify Him? My prayer is that you should grasp this insight regarding the Name of *God*. The Bible gives us revelation into what *God* is like. Open your mind to some non-conventional thinking about this *Being* we call *God*. First of all, *God* is unconditioned consciousness. By this, I mean *He* is consciousness without boundaries or limits. Contemplate or consider *'Unconditioned Consciousness'* now. Meditate quietly on and consider unlimited consciousness.

God is the ALL-MIGHTY Supreme Being.

God is Infinite Intelligence.

God is 'I AM'.

'I AM' is God.

God is Unconditioned Consciousness.

Now, let us move into the realm of 'I AM'. Meditate on the words 'I AM'. This is a wonderful way to practice 'I AM' consciousness. Just assume, meditate, and contemplate, considering the 'I AM' state of *Being*. Remain in this state of consciousness. As you do, your outer world of prosperity will reflect this. This is because *God's* Name is powerful and it will out-picture or manifest prosperity when you have faith in that Name.

GOD'S NAME

In Jewish thought, a name is not merely an arbitrary designation. The name conveys the nature and essence of the thing named. It represents the history and reputation of the thing named. So, what is the significance of the Name of God? First of all, God's Name is 'I AM or Jehovah'.

How does the names 'I AM' and Jehovah relate? That is a good question. The Name Jehovah means; *'I AM The One Who Is'*. So then Jehovah literally means 'I AM the Self-Existent One' or I AM BEING.

Let's dig into this Name a little deeper. The name Jehovah is represented by the four Hebrew letters **Yod-Heh-Vav-Heh**(YHVH). It is often referred to in Judaism as the 'Unutterable Name'. In Scripture, this Name is used when discussing *God's* relationship to humanity, and when emphasizing *His* qualities of loving-kindness and mercy.

YHVH

In studying *God's* Name a good and clear example is in **Exodus 3:14** where Moses asked *God* what *His* Name is. He is not asking what should I call you; rather he is asking; God, *Who are you? What are you like? What have you done?* This is clear from *God's* response which was *"I AM THAT I AM."*

In Exodus 3:14 we get the 'I AM' insight. The most important of *God's* Names is the four-letter Name represented by the Hebrew letters YOD-HEH-VAV-HEY*(YHVH)*.

According to Hebrew scholars, the meaning of YOD-HEH-VAV-HEY*(YHVH)* reflects the fact that *God's* existence is eternal and literally means *'I AM THAT I AM'*. Notice how all roads take us back to 'I AM'. The simple sum of the matter is that *God's* Name is 'I AM'.

THE REDEMPTIVE NAMES

So now, let us look at the eight compound Names of Jehovah as revealed in scripture. Let us Visualize, Affirm and Meditate on the Names and redemptive benefits to you. Visualize the benefit(s) manifesting for you. Boldly make the affirmation. Meditate on the end result.

THE NAMES & THE REDEMPTIVE BENEFITS

Jehovah-Tsidkenu   "I AM YOUR RIGHTEOUSNESS"

Affirmation: *I AM free from Sin*

Jehovah-M'Kaddesh   "I AM YOUR SANCTIFICATION"

Affirmation: *I AM free from Condemnation*

Jehovah-Shalom   "I AM YOUR PEACE"

Affirmation: *I AM filled with the Spirit*

Jehovah-Shammah   "I AM EVER PRESENT"

Affirmation: *I AM a partaker of the Divine Nature*

Jehovah-Rohi   "I AM YOUR SHEPHERD"

Affirmation: *I AM under Divine care and security*

Jehovah-Nissi   "I AM YOUR BANNER"

Affirmation: *I AM living in Love's Victory*

Jehovah-Rophe   "I AM YOUR HEALER"

Affirmation: *I AM free from sickness... sound!*

Jehovah-Jireh   "I AM YOUR PROVIDER"

Affirmation: *I AM free from failure...success!*

God's Name must *Be-Being Hallowed!* He is the Beginning and the End! *He* is the Great 'I AM'! Amen!

SHARING 'I AM'

So, you have found 'I AM'. Which means that you are truly blessed! You can't find the powerful, positive, life-changing truth of 'I AM' and not share this with others. *WHEN YOU FIND I AM, YOU MUST SHARE I AM.*

So, you have found *Him, haven't you?* Now share *Him* by sharing the knowledge you have gotten.

Please share this book with at least one other person. To obtain more copies go to <u>www.atlantanewthought.com</u>

Thank you!

Blessing & Peace,

Bernard.

'I AM' JOURNAL

_____

_____

_____

_____

_____

_____

_____

_____

_____

_____

_____

_____

_____

_____

_____

_____

_____

_____

FINAL WORDS

'I AM' is the greatest affirmation you can make because 'I AM' is *God*, and *God* is Love. *He* came in Jesus Christ as the fulfilling of the Law. Love is the fulfilling of the law, and the Law of love dominates.

Love never fails!

Love is our victory!

'I AM' is our victory!

'I AM' is the power and presence of love!

'I AM' NEVER FAILS!

MY PRAYER FOR YOU

'May the LORD bless you and keep you.

May the LORD smile down on you and show you his kindness.

May the LORD answer your prayers and give you peace.'

Please subscribe to my website for a downloadable FREE gift at: www.atlantanewthought.com

APPENDIX: THE VAM WORKSHOP

Make each affirmation for 30 days. Visualize, Affirm, and Meditate on Prosperity.

#1 VAM! AFFIRMATIONS TO ATTRACT WEALTH

I am open to receiving wealth.

I am attracting great wealth into my life.

I am a magnet for wealth.

Wealth flows to me and through me.

Wealth comes to me in different ways.

Attracting wealth comes easily and effortlessly to me.

I believe that I can easily attract wealth.

I am naturally drawn to wealth.

Being wealthy is my birthright.

I am surrounded by wealth and riches.

VAM PERSONAL WEALTH JOURNAL

_____

_____

_____

_____

_____

_____

_____

_____

_____

_____

_____

_____

_____

_____

_____

_____

_____

_____

_____

_____

_____

#2 VAM! AFFIRMATIONS TO ATTRACT PROSPERITY

I am attracting prosperity every day.

I am capable of manifesting prosperity in my life.

I am grateful for my prosperity.

I easily create abundance and prosperity.

I have a right to be rich and prosperous.

I have a constant flow of money.

Success and prosperity are all around me.

I am attracting great financial opportunities.

I believe in my abilities to attract financial prosperity.

Being rich and prosperous is natural to me.

I am prosperity!

VAM PERSONAL WEALTH JOURNAL

_____

_____

_____

_____

_____

_____

_____

_____

_____

_____

_____

_____

_____

_____

_____

_____

_____

_____

_____

_____

#3 VAM AFFIRMATIONS TO ATTRACT MORE INCOME

I am determined to attract more income.

I am attracting greater and greater financial opportunities.

I am increasing my income every day.

My bank account is flowing with income.

The money I give comes back to me in multiples.

I believe I can create stronger financial stability.

I find it easy to attract more income.

Money comes to me constantly and effortlessly.

My actions attract a bigger income every day.

VAM PERSONAL WEALTH JOURNAL

_____

_____

_____

_____

_____

_____

_____

_____

_____

_____

_____

_____

_____

_____

_____

_____

_____

_____

_____

_____

_____

_____

#4 VAM AFFIRMATIONS TO DESERVE WEALTH AND PROSPERITY

I am worthy of abundance and prosperity.

I am worthy of having financial stability.

I am worthy of being rich, successful, and wealthy.

I deserve good things in my life.

I let go of my money restrictions.

I release my resistance to wealth.

I deserve to enjoy financial abundance.

I deserve to be financially free.

VAM PERSONAL WEALTH JOURNAL

#5 VAM AFFIRMATIONS FOR 'I AM' CONSCIOUSNESS

"I am open and ready to attract abundance into my life."

"I am attuned to the frequency of love and abundance."

"I am open to receiving limitless abundance."

"I am wealthy. I attract success."

"I am living in a consciousness of complete abundance."

"I am radiating abundance."

"I am living a life of abundance."

"I am a prosperity magnet."

"I am living in the overflow of prosperity."

"I am attracting money easily and effortlessly."

"I am increasingly magnetic to wealth, abundance, prosperity, and money."

"I am attracting more and more abundance into my life every day."

"I am living a life of unlimited abundance."

"I am flowing in the abundance that is all around me."

"I am affluent. I have an abundance mindset."

"I am abundance!"

VAM PERSONAL WEALTH JOURNAL

AUTHOR BIO

Bernard Smalls is a transformational teacher who has functioned as a corporate trainer in the business world and as a consulting resource with a focus on leadership, sales, and service excellence. Bernard teaches spiritual and practical principles which he calls 'spiritual-pragmatism'. In a previous career, he was a professional drummer playing in the Oakland-San Francisco Bay Area. After a potentially lucrative deal with Motown fell through, he began to pursue spiritual development. Bernard is a student of Psychology and holds a Bachelor's Degree in Esoteric Theology. He embraces an interfaith approach to spirituality and is the founder of the Atlanta New Thought and the Atlanta Centre for I AM. He can be heard daily on I AM Positive Thinking Internet Radio at www.atlantanewthought.com

Bernard Smalls, Author

CONTACT ME

Bernard@atlantanewthought.com

P.O. BOX 724

SUWANEE, GA. 30024

PH. 678-382-1556

Subscribe for our free digital motivational gift at www.atlantanewthought.com

Made in the USA
Las Vegas, NV
29 May 2021

23854869R00080